THE
LAST
GREAT
SPIRITUAL
CONFLICT

A Vision
and
Two Prophecies

Michael D. Fortner

Trumpet Press, Lawton, OK

Abbreviations & Volumes Used:

MEV – Modern English Version (based on the Textus Receptus)

Author: D. Fortner, Michael
Title: The Last Great Spiritual Conflict
1. Pentecostalism 2. Visions and prophecy 3. Pentecostal history 4. Word of Faith 5. Heresy

ISBN: 979-898-700-091-5

Learn about future books by the author at
www.michaelfortner.com

Trumpet Press is a member of the Christian Indie Publishing Association (CIPA).

Other books by Michael D. Fortner:

Satan's False Prophets Exposed
Editing God: Textual Criticism and Modern Bibles Analyzed
Pentecostal Newspapers: Messengers of An Outpouring

Books only available on the author's website (in March 2023):
Bible Prophecy Revealed: 2023
The Fall of Babylon and The Final Antichrist: 2023
The Approaching Apocalypse and Three Days of Darkness: 2023

www.usbibleprophecy.com and www.michaelfortner.com

Table of Contents

Introduction

In 1916, a vision was published in *The Weekly Evangel*, the newspaper of the Assembly of God; this vision showed that two great attacks would come upon the Pentecostals. The first one was an external attack which was successfully repelled. The second attack was to come from the inside! The elements of the vision point to this attack as being the rise of the Word of Faith movement.

Christians around the world are going through a great end-time spiritual battle right now; but they are mostly unaware of a great deception that has come into a large part of the Pentecostal movement over the past 60 years.

This book is about that attack; the battle between traditional Pentecostals and Charismatics, and the Word of Faith Movement.

Chapter One discusses the vision and how it is being played out today. Chapter Two discusses two important prophecies that relate to this save inside attack, with examples of some of the false teachings of the WOF movement.

Chapter Three gives some articles and testimonies found in the Pentecostal newspapers of 100+ years ago that show great miracles and signs and wonders that took place, proving that they had great faith and did great things for God. Contrary to the slander made by the WOF teachers that those Pentecostals believed in poverty, and lacked faith.

It is sad that so many Pentecostals do not even know what the Word of Faith movement is, or what they teach compared to historic Pentecostalism. This lack of understanding that they are not the same, has led many to listen to and be deceived by these wolves in sheep's clothing.

There are manifestations within the WOF movement which never occurred among the early Pentecostals. The Pentecostals never had dog barking, or chicken clucking as manifestations, which happens in some WOF churches. I explain why. Whereas, the Pentecostals had manifestations which rarely happen today.

This is a short book, but it packs a punch!

Chapter One

A Vision of The

Last Great Spiritual Conflict

July 29, 1916.   THE WEEKLY EVANGEL   Page Five.

THE LAST GREAT SPIRITUAL CONFICT.

A Vision.

Evangelist Fred Eiting sends us the account of a vision which he had some time ago, as follows:

"I was in deep earnest prayer and had been searching the Word of God and the coming of the Lord was made very real to me. I was made to see that we are in the last days and that perilous times are upon us, and that 'because iniquity shall abound the love of many shall wax cold.' A holy longing and determination filled my heart that I might not fail the Master, but be true to Jesus at all cost. One night the Spirit of the Lord was heavily upon me and during prayer the following vision was given to me:—

I saw myself with a vast army, mounted upon large white horses. We followed a captain who was also mounted upon a very beautiful white horse. My attention was first drawn to our apparel. All were clothed with white robes. "What can this mean?" I thought. Immediately I saw all were warriors and had on full armor underneath their white robes. I could see their swords and shields. We were riding through a desert country but all seemed to be filled with joy to be counted worthy to follow so great a leader. All were in perfect harmony. We felt so secure and peaceful and courageous as we followed in close line. Every man knew his orders, but the principal command seemed to be to follow our captain and to keep our whole attention upon Him. Presently in the distance I saw a great army of horsemen coming toward us, and as they drew nearer I observed that instead of being clothed in white robes they were clothed in black and were riding black horses. They were com-

speech. I could see these begin to weaken and lose courage. The arm that had wielded the sword against the enemy became powerless and their shields became heavy and began to lower, their swords finally falling to the ground, and, in this condition, I saw the awful attack of the enemy upon them as they pierced them as with a dart and they would fall helpless, from their horses. Often we would surround a helpless brother and try to assist him to mount again and join the ranks and some were able to gather courage and take their places again, while others were so weak and sickened they fainted by the way never to rise again.

Our time was limited. We could not tarry long in assisting the fallen, for our great Commander's orders were to move forward and keep our eyes upon Him. However, as a fallen brother would rise and again take his place there was real rejoicing. We seemed now to understand the plan of the enemy better and with a greater determination gave no place for him in our ranks, but seemed to feel we were each other's keepers and were bound together by cords of love, perfectly confident that our great Captain was able to take us through more than conquerors. "Behold I have given him for a commander to the people." Isa. 55:4. See Rev. 19:11 to 20.

"In conclusion, strengthen yourselves in the Lord and in the power which His supreme might imparts. Put on the complete armor of God, so as to be able to stand firm against all the stratagems of the devil. For ours is not a conflict with mere flesh and blood but with despotisms, the empires, the forces that control and govern this dark world—the spiritual hosts of evil arrayed against us in the heavenly warfare."—Weymouth.

Here is the text of the vision as it appeared in *The Weekly Evangel*, in 1916, but it was seen an unknown number of months or years prior. It describes two attacks; the first one was fulfilled within a short time. The second attack began a few decades later; and we are still living with the results; this is why the vision is important for us today; we are still in this great battle, and we need to finally win it, once and for all. But we cannot do so, unless we are aware of what the enemy has done and is doing. This vision will give us much information about this battle which we need to know in order to fight the enemy of our souls. Here is the text of the article:—

Evangelist Fred Eiting sends us the account of a vision which he had some time ago, as follows:—

* * * * * * *

I was in deep earnest prayer and had been searching the Word of God and the coming of the Lord was made very real to me. I was made to see that we are in the last days and that perilous times are upon us, and that "because iniquity shall abound, the love of many shall wax cold." A holy longing and determination filled my heart that I might not fail the Master, but be true to Jesus at all cost. One night the Spirit of the Lord was heavily upon me and during prayer the following vision was given to me:--

I saw myself with a vast army, mounted upon large white horses. We followed a captain who was also mounted upon a very beautiful white horse. My attention was first drawn to our apparel. All were clothed with white robes. "What can this mean?" I thought. Immediately I saw all were warriors and had on full armor underneath their white robes. I could see their swords and shields. We were riding through a desert country but all seemed to be filled with joy to be counted worthy to follow so great a leader. All were in perfect harmony. We felt so secure and peaceful and courageous as we followed in close line. Every man knew his orders, but the principal command seemed to be to follow our captain and to keep our whole attention upon Him.

Presently, in the distance I saw a great army of horsemen coming toward us, and as they drew nearer I observed that instead of being clothe in white robes they were clothed in black and were riding black horses. They were coming toward us at full speed. Their faces were very fierce and they presented a frightful aspect, but I observed they had no armor on and carried no shields, as did our army. Their only weapon was a long spear.

All realized that a battle was imminent and felt it was a decisive and final one. We looked at each other and I could see some in our ranks turn pale. Others were so frightened they seemed ready to turn back, and as we looked into His glorious face, all fear left us and strength and courage came in its place. His very countenance seemed to express His will and desire for us. We were filled with the consciousness that our mighty leader was facing the foe and that the brunt of the battle was against Him. The thought that the enemy must first overcome Him gave us great courage.

The two vast hosts met and it seemed at first we would be trampled under their feet. But just here a wonderful thing happened. Our leader pierced the ranks of the enemy and we were led victoriously through the center of that great dark host. The enemy was dismayed, frightened, utterly confounded at their being suddenly repulsed and at the bold victory of our Captain. Realizing their utter defeat they turned and rode alongside of our army seeking to overcome us in a different manner.

Our soldiers, seeming to understand the change in their tactics, refused to make friends with them, fought with their swords and defeated the enemy on every hand, as they were without shield and were exposed to our attacks. After a time, the conflict seemed to turn into a battle of words and strife. Again and again, I heard the black riders say, "If you will not follow us or become one with us, please don't fight us. We want to make friends with you." But I noticed many of our soldiers refusing to make friends with them and continuing to wield their swords with great courage and indignation, cutting right and left into the ranks of the enemy. Others left off fighting and listened to their cunning and deceptive speech.

I could see these begin to weaken and lose courage. The arm that had wielded the sword against the enemy became powerless and their shields became heavy and began to lower; their swords finally falling to the ground, and, in this condition, I saw the awful attack of the enemy upon them as they pierced them as with a dart and they would fall helpless from their horses. Often we would surround a helpless brother and try to assist him to mount again and join the ranks and some were able to gather courage and take their places again, while others were so weak and sickened they fainted by the way, never to rise again.

Our time was limited. We could not tarry long in assisting the fallen, for our great Commander's orders were to move forward and keep our eyes upon Him. However, as a fallen brother would rise and again take his place, there was real rejoicing. We seemed now to understand the plan of the enemy better and with a greater determination, gave no place for him in our ranks, but seemed to feel we were each other's keepers and were bound together by cords of love, perfectly confident that our great Captain was able to take us through more than conquerors. "Behold I have given him a commander to the people." Isa. 55; Rev. 19:11-20.

In conclusion, "strengthen yourselves in the Lord and in the power which His supreme might imparts. Put on the complete armor of God, so as to be able to stand firm against all the stratagems of the devil. For ours is not a conflict with mere flesh and blood but with despotisms, the empires, the forces that control and govern this dark world -- the spiritual hosts of evil arrayed against us in the heavenly warfare." (July 29, 1916)

* * * * * * *

The first attack against the Pentecostal people was from the outside which the enemy did not win; so they changed tactics and began riding alongside of us; in this way they began making many of us believe that they were with us. This tells me that the second attack will arise from within Pentecostalism by preaching and teaching false doctrines. People who believe those lies will become spiritually weak and defeated by Satan.

It is likely that the first assault which Jesus broke through was the great amount of false teachings which arose and threatened the movement in the early years. These false teachings were a major factor in the formation of Pentecostal denominations, so they could control the doctrines. They formed a united force against the attacks.

Here is an except from an article in *The Latter Rain Evangel*, titled; *"God's Word versus Man's Word, A Candid Criticism of Spurious Writings"*:

> This article will deal with a matter that has been stealthily encroaching upon the Pentecostal assemblies, preying upon the credulity of well-meaning and simple hearted people who honestly desire more of God. We feel it is time to speak out and warn those who are being seduced by so-called prophetic utterances purporting to be the voice of God coming with the authority of sacred Scripture. We refer to the books entitled, "In School with the Holy Ghost," "Honey out of the Rock," and the "Letters from Jesus." The instructions, rebukes and "prophetic" utterances are for the most part so utterly absurd and foolish it seems a waste of time to answer them, but precious souls are being led astray and the cause of Christ is brought into disrepute. . . . (page 13)

> Now a word as to the teaching of these books on sin. We confess to being shocked by this way of dealing with sin. It seems akin to Christian Science which teaches that sin is made null to us by a denial of its reality. The following passages are selected from Book Five:

> "That which is wrong in you is not yours. It is not counted to you. You are not under any responsibility for it. . . . I in My death dealt with every wrong thought. So then, when wrong thoughts come there is no condemnation for them. . . . You have no sin, the sin that lieth in you is not yours. . . . The old nature in you that won't behave and won't be free and good, is nothing that you need to be condemned for. . . ." (page 17)

> Nothing brings such discredit to the cause of Christ and keeps outsiders from entering in to salvation as to see Christians professing a holiness they do not have in their daily walk, and nothing so shuts believers out from the realization of true holiness as resting in the false assumption that the sin they commit is not theirs. . . . On page 69 is the following:

> "You can't think wrong for I am thinking for you. You can't be wrong for I am being for you." (*TLRE*, Dec., 1912, p. 17)

* * * * *

This sounds a lot like New Age mumbo-jumbo teaching. But that falsehood did not get a foothold in the Pentecostal movement, so it was successfully defeated. Those books cannot even be found online today. Because of Satan's defeat, he decided to change his plan of attack. Here are some important points from the vision:

> . . . they turned and <u>rode alongside of our army</u> seeking to overcome us in a different manner. . . . the conflict seemed to turn into <u>a battle of words and strife</u>. . . . "If you will not follow us or become one with us, <u>please don't fight us</u>. We want to make friends with you." . . . left off fighting and <u>listened to their cunning and deceptive speech</u>.

This vision happened over 110 years ago; this means this attack has already happened, and it was successful! <u>This shows us false teaching rising up within the Pentecostal movement.</u>

This false movement has already spread inside Pentecostalism. Notice that the vision said the battle was one of "<u>*words* *and strife*</u>." This refers to the "Word of Faith" movement that was started by Kenneth Hagin in the 1950s, who was an Assembly of God preacher. He taught that it was all about your words, that you should claim how much money you need, confess what you want, and you will get it. He wrote a little book called "*You Can Have What You Say.*" He said you can get whatever you want from God; all you have to do is follow the steps he gave which was mainly saying what you wanted out-loud, and you actually had to tell people in order for it to work.

In the vision, the false brethren said, "*don't fight us*," and "*we want to be friends*." Paul Crouch was the son of an AOG missionary, but he swallowed WOF doctrine whole and pushed it on TBN. He would get on TV and complain about what he called "heresy hunters" who were pointing out the gross errors in WOF teaching. He would say that they should not attack the WOF doctrine or preachers; why not just let the teachers teach what they want and let God sort it out when we get to heaven? In other words, *"don't fight us,"* and, *"let's be friends."*

There was a time when I watched TBN, and as it happened, I was watching the Praise the Lord, Praise-a-Thon on April 2, 1991. I did not realize that 30 years later I would need to reference the statements Paul Crouch made, but fortunately, Hank Hanegraaff documented it in his book, *Christianity in Crisis: 21ˢᵗ Century.* Paul specifically said:

> . . . let God "sort out all this doctrinal doo-doo. . . . Who cares? Let Jesus sort that all out at the judgment seat of Christ. We'll find out who was right and wrong doctrinally." (page 233)

If you are pointing out someone's heresy, you are not walking in love, right? Kenneth Hagin believed that his formula did not work unless you walk in love, sounds good, right? *Yum.* On another PTL program, his son said this about him:

> I have never heard him say anything bad about anybody. In fact, people would come and ask him about some things [about other people], and he might know something about something; after they would leave, mother would say, "Why didn't you tell them something so they wouldn't get in trouble?" He said, "well, I don't want anything to come out of my mouth against anybody else. I'll pray that the Lord will direct them," and he said "I don't believe it's my responsibility speak bad about anybody." (*PTL* program, April 23, 1998, Youtube.com)

So, supposedly it is not love to speak the truth or to point out that so-and-so is a false teacher! YES, it is, what is NOT LOVE is to allow people to be deceived and do nothing to warn them when you know that they are being deceived. The devil does not want people speaking out against his false teachers! The Apostle Paul and the early Pentecostals spoke out against false teachers!

Why was I watching TBN in 1991? Most Pentecostals were watching and becoming slowly deceived. At that time they did not understand the dangers. Because of this army of false teachers that arose, many Christians have let down their weapons and have been overcome by the enemy, just as seen in the vision. It has greatly weakened the entire Pentecostal movement, and is threatening to take it over, at least in the USA.

David Wilkerson warned us in the 1980s to get rid of our televisions, but he was attacked as being an extremist. "No, what about Christian TV?" Well, it turns out we would have been much better off had we not watched Christian TV!

Thanks to Pentecostals sending in their money, today the WOF has become powerful and controls many churches and the majority of the Pentecostal/ Charismatic mass-media. No religious program is allowed to be on TBN that speaks against WOF. Most spirit-filled pastors who do not specifically teach WOF doctrine will not dare speak against the movement, and will even invite WOF preachers to speak in their churches.

But you cannot hug a pig without getting stink and filth on you. They hug them like they are one of them because they want to be guests on their TV shows to talk about their latest book. If they speak the truth, then they will be cut-off from 75-80% of the Christian(?) media.

Satan is the prince of the power of the air, and he controls the majority of the mass media, including the "Christian" media. So he promotes his false teachers to prominent positions and does his best to attack the truth. Because of these big name preachers on TBN, there are many people teaching that you should be wealthy. Fred Price (1932-2021) was a follower of Hagin and had a show on TBN and said, *"I drive a Rolls Royce -- I'm following Jesus' steps"* (Hanegraaff, page 58). He was as big a deceiver as Kenneth Hagin.

Hagin and Crouch smeared and slandered the early Pentecostals by their false statements about them. They claimed they taught a Gospel of poverty, and that Hagin was the father of faith, but both claims are false. I recently published a book with 500 pages of articles and testimonies from early Pentecostalism which show that they did great things for God.

It takes great faith to start on a trip around the world with 28 cents in your pocket; but that is exactly what Daniel Awrey did. And not because he was broke, but because that is what God told him to do. But even that takes great faith. And in every church he spoke in, he never once asked for a dime, but all his needs were met (*Pentecostal Newspapers: Messengers of an Outpouring*).

Another preacher took his family to the train station with no money at all, and yet they traveled by train to another city where he started a new work, and one year later he had built a church that was paid for. Many other evangelists bought tents, and traveled all across the US preaching in cities and small towns. They had many revivals with many saved and healed; and many churches were started.

The pages of those papers record many great miracles, and revivals lasting for longer than the Brownsville Revival in Pensacola in the 1990s. Healings took place nightly, blind eyes opened, the lame walked, people dying of cancer were instantly healed. People who were barely alive were carried into the tents and left walking and running!

So, DON'T YOU DARE SLANDER the early Pentecostals!!

Some of them were indeed poor, but they were no less well-off than most other Americans of the time. My grandmother was born in 1901 in central Oklahoma. When they heard about the outpouring at Azusa Street, her older sister and her husband traveled there, and got the baptism, and were called by God to be missionaries to the Middle East, and went.

So, even though some of them were poor, it is very clear that they actually had GREAT FAITH. It is difficult to live by faith when you have a bank account full of money. Relying on God for your daily needs requires strong faith.

Nor did they teach poverty, but what they did NOT teach is that God wants you rich! The Pentecostal newspapers have

many testimonies about miracles of provision. The early Pentecostals were able to build many churches and support many
missionaries because they gave what they had in faith, and
God met the needs.

But Hagin was a failed pastor and evangelist! He said in the
video (*Praise the Lord* TV program, April 23, 1998, You
tube.com), that he pastored four churches in 12 years, but his
own website says he pastored five churches in 12 years. Why
were there no big revivals in any of them?

If Hagin had the power of God working in his ministry like
any of those dozens of early Pentecostal evangelists, he would
have been a great success. After pastoring, he became an evangelist for a year and wore out a car and had to sell it for junk to
pay some of his bills, and was on foot. He was a failure until he
began teaching his false doctrine. With Hagin, it was not about
the power of God but the "words" you spoke. This is what
Hagin said on TBN:

> The Lord said to me, "Don't pray for finances anymore, or
> money like you have." . . . I said, "What do I do?" He said,
> "Number one you claim what you need." . . . It took $150 a
> week to meet my budget, "Alright, then you claim that." . . .
> He said, "The money's not up here, I'm not going to send
> any raining down from heaven, I'd have to counterfeit and
> I'm not a counterfeiter, its down there. . . . And it's not me
> that's withholding from your children, it's Satan, the god of
> this world. You first claim what you need or want." And
> then he said, "You say, 'Satan take your hands off my mon-
> ey.' And then you say, 'Go ministering spirits and cause it to
> come.'" (Ibid)

From that time onward he no longer prayed to God about
money, but claimed the amount he wanted-- from Satan. He
said God said, "*It is not me that is withholding it from your children, it's Satan.*" So we are expected to believe that Satan is
stronger than God, and is keeping money from us! But that is
false. It is true that Satan can attack our finances in the same
way that he can attack our bodies with sickness; but when that

happens, the correct response is the same; rebuke the attack in the name of Jesus!

Satan is NOT in control of your finances! Think about what he said. He claims that God said;

> "The money's not up here, I'm not going to send any raining down from heaven, . . . it's not me that's withholding from your children, it's Satan, the god of this world. You first claim what you need or want."

In other words, *"I don't have your money, Satan does, get it from him!"* Hagin wants us to believe that Satan is the one who is in control of all the money in the world; that our prosperity comes from Satan! LIE. Here is what we learn from the above information:

1. Hagin no longer prayed to God for money.
2. Hagin told Satan how much money he needed each week.
3. Hagin commanded "spirits" to go and cause the money to come to him.

That should send chills down your spine. The Bible says God will supply all of our needs, not Satan! It also says God will *"open you the windows of heaven, and pour you out a blessing"* but according to Hagin, there is nothing up there for us down here?

Oral Roberts started out as a true minister of God, but swallowed the WOF doctrine and became a false teacher. In addition to the prosperity gospel, he taught a fake Holy Spirit baptism. There was a time when I sent Oral money to support his TV program and build his hospital that was not finished and had to be sold, because he could not afford to finish and run it. On his TV show he taught people to just say whatever gobbledygook they want to say, and that is your prayer language; and then whatever you say next in English is the interpretation! COUNTERFEIT!

It is true that you can speak in tongues at-will once you get the real baptism, which is then the Spirit praying (1 Cor. 14:2).

That is different from giving out a message in tongues during a service, which is followed by the interpretation. But Oral's teaching had people believing they were praying in tongues when they were not. This is deception from the pit of hell. Kenneth Copeland teaches the same lie. I have seen videos of other WOF preachers who appear to be speaking in fake tongues. I grew up attending a Pentecostal church, so I usually tell the genuine from the fake.

His son Richard teaches that if you are born again, then you already have the Holy Spirit, and there is no need for a separate baptism in the Holy Spirit. He then proceeds to teach those in the congregation he is speaking to, how to speak in tongues. He said in a video:

> How many of you are born again; let me see your hands? Then you have the Holy Spirit. Now, you may not be taking advantage of Him; you may not be allowing Him to speak through you, but you have Him.

This is FAKE, COUNTERFEIT! Satan does not want you to have the genuine baptism in the Holy Spirit, which is additional power! He can be seen on videos teaching this on Youtube.

Also, notice that not only are "words" emphasized in this movement, but the vision said, "*a battle of words and strife.*" That same word, "strife," as a verb is "strive," which is defined as:

> to try very hard to do something or to make something happen, especially for a long time or against difficulties. (dictionary. cambridge. org)

This is exactly what WOF teaches regarding saying confessions, that you have to confess it for many months and years until you finally get it. In other words, strive for it. Striving is not Faith. WOF teaches that you can make things happen with the words of your mouth. Hagin taught people to claim what they want, "*that house is mine*" (*You Can Have What You Say*), even if the owner does not want to sell, if you claim it, it will become yours; you just have to keep confessing it until you finally get it. Joel Osteen is also a WOF preacher, known for his false teaching.

I found an official position statement on the Assembly of God website by the title, *"the Believer and Positive Confession (Adopted by the General Presbytery in session August 19, 1980)"* (seen in August 2022). This statement appears to speak against WOF doctrines, but it does not actually contain the words "Word of Faith," and is not even well written. Someone could easily read the statement and come away believing that it is only speaking against "extremes" of the WOF teaching. Here are a few excerpts:

> The Assemblies of God from its early days has recognized the importance of the life of faith. It has been given prominent emphasis because Scripture gives it prominence. . . . it is important for believers to be mindful of the example in Scripture of being strong in faith (Romans 4:20-24). They must be on guard against anything which would weaken or destroy faith. . . .

> Occasionally throughout church history people have taken extreme positions concerning great Biblical truths. . . .

> The fact that extremes are brought into focus does not imply rejection of the doctrine of confession. It is an important truth. The Bible teaches people are to confess their sin (1 John 1:9). They are to confess Christ (Matthew 10:32; Romans 10:9, 10).They are to maintain a good confession (Hebrews 4:14; 10:23, ASV). . . .

> [About positive confession]: This view goes a step further and divides confession into negative and positive aspects. The negative is acknowledging sin, sickness, poverty, or other undesirable situations. Positive confession is acknowledging or owning desirable situations. . . .

> According to this view, as expressed in various publications, the believer who refrains from acknowledging the negative and continues to affirm the positive will as sure for himself

pleasant circumstances. He will be able to rule over poverty, disease, and sickness. He will be sick only if he confesses he is sick. Some make a distinction between acknowledging the symptoms of an illness and the illness itself.

This view advocates that God wants believers to wear the best clothing, drive the best cars, and have the best of everything. Believers need not suffer financial setbacks. All they need to do is to tell Satan to take his hands off their money. The believer can have whatever he says whether the need is spiritual, physical, or financial. It is taught that faith compels God's action.

You can read the entire statement by Googling, Assemblies of God (USA), *The Believer and Positive Confession*. Unfortunately, it does not take a clear stand and actually name the Word of Faith. It should clearly state whether it is speaking against the WOF movement or just extremes in the WOF movement.

The early Pentecostals had such great faith, I would compare them to Samson; but those in the WOF are like limp dishrags. I saw a video of Kenneth Copeland laying hands on people at one of his huge conventions and the people not only DID NOT GET HEALED, but they did not even react to any anointing or power; his hand may as well have been dead (*Kenneth Copeland and Oral Roberts brag about being rich*, You tube.com). He had no anointing.

There is not room in this book to discuss all the false WOF doctrines in detail, for that I recommend *Christianity in Crisis for the 21st Century*, and *A Different Gospel* by Dan R. McConnell, and *Preachers of a Different Gospel*, by Femi Adeleye. In my own book, *Satan's False Prophets Exposed*, there are a few chapters about WOF doctrine, but it also covers other related areas. There are also several books specifically against the prosperity gospel, which is the most widely spread WOF teaching, and has infiltrated many denominations.

But I feel compelled to mention a few of the greatly blasphemous statements. Kenneth Copeland said, "*God is the biggest failure in the Bible,*" (found many places online); and he called

Jesus a, "*little wormy spirit*". Copeland even said that if he, <u>Ken-neth Copeland, had been alive 2,000 years ago, that he could have died for the sins of the world</u>. If you do not know how crazy-wrong that statement is, you need to learn the basic doc-trines of Christianity. If Copeland were alive 2,000 years ago, he would likely have been Judas.

This is because WOF doctrine teaches that Jesus was an ordinary man who went to hell (he did not even go to Paradise, but hell!) and yet was reborn in hell by the Holy Spirit-- LIE. <u>WOF teaches that the death of Jesus on the cross could not have paid for anyone's sin</u> (just ignore what the Bible clearly says), but that he had to suffer in hell to pay for your sins-- LIE.

Hanegraaff says Hagin, "*vociferously proclaimed that the physi-cal death of Christ was insufficient to atone for sin*" (*Christianity in Crisis: 21st Century*, page 180)

They believe that Jesus was an ordinary man who was born again in hell. Creflo Dollar said, "*He was actually the first person to ever become born again*" (Ibid, page 184). <u>This is the worst heresy that could ever be taught</u>. The Bible clearly says that Je-sus paid for your sin by his "blood" (Acts 20:28, Colossians 1:20, Ephesians 1:7 , Hebrews 9:22, 1 John 1:7). And the rea-son his blood paid for your sin is because he was the SON OF GOD.

I believe Satan targeted Ken Hagin because he was stupid; all you have to do is read some of his teaching to understand he was stupid. He said you needed to have faith in your faith, and you cannot be saved unless you actually "hear" the Gospel with your ears. Because of his stupidity, he was fooled into be-lieving Satan's lies, which he then spread among many full-gospel believers. WOF preachers likely have millions of follow-ers! *Blind leading the blind.*

Considering how grossly deceived the WOF are, it should come as no surprise the Kenneth Copeland is lovey-dovey with the Charismatic Renewal within the Roman Catholic Church; and even helps finance Tony Palmer, who is an emissary between the WOF and the RCC. You can see Kenneth Copeland and Tony Palmer standing next to Pope Francis in photos.

Not to be outdone, Creflo Dollar has endorsed and encouraged his church members to vote for Stacey Abrams when she ran for governor in 2022. She supports abortion up to the moment of birth. She also supports Critical Race Theory and other godless lies. (www.charismanews.com)

Many times, a false teacher will gradually begin to teach more and more false doctrine over time. Creflo has long been one of the most extreme prosperity preachers. In 2022 he said he no longer believed that tithing was a correct, Biblical teaching.

Pentecostals never taught his WOF prosperity gospel, but they have always believed in tithing, even before Pentecostal denominations were formed. One of the main reasons was that Abraham paid tithes to Melchizedek long before the Law of Moses.

Many false teachers just cannot believe what is true; they must teach one false doctrine or another. Most of these WOF teachers teach a boat-load of false, twisted, and outlandish invented doctrines. Yet, Christians keep sending them millions of dollars. The false WOF preachers will gradually go farther and farther away from the truth. A video showed Creflo Dollar standing in his church, and he said:

> I just want to say this because I want to see how it sounds, *Governor Stacey Abrams* just walked in. I'm so glad to see you again. . . . So you already know what to do, right? How many of you have already done it? . . . Make it happen.

(Nov. 7., *This Is Why You Never TEST God*; the channel is Gospel of Christ.) She was running for governor of the state of Georgia in 2022. Creflo was telling his people to go out and vote for a woman who supports killing babies up to the moment of birth, and Critical Race Theory. Think about that! A man who claims to preach the Gospel, supporting the murder of babies, and hate for whites.

Chapter Two

Two Prophecies

In 1965, Stanley H. Frodsham, retired editor of the *Pentecostal Evangel*, gave a prophecy at *Elim Bible Institute* which is still widely available online; in this prophecy, he said there were coming teachers who would <u>begin teaching gross heresy after they became well-known ministers</u>. And that <u>God would actually anoint these ministers</u>, because God will use them to *"purify and sift"* his people. In other words, "test."

As God's timing would have it, after I first wrote the last chapter, I came across Stanley Frodsham's prophecy, which I had read at least twice before in the past 20 years; but I had forgotten the details. As I read it again, I saw clearly that part of it fit exactly the WOF founders and leaders today:

> But I warn you of seducing spirits who instruct My people in an evil way. Many of these <u>I shall anoint</u>, that they may <u>purify and sift</u> My people; for I would have a holy people. . .
> .
>
> There shall come deceivers among My people in increasing numbers, who shall speak forth the truth and shall gain the favour of the people. For the people shall examine the Scriptures and say, 'What these men say is true'. Then <u>when they have gained the hearts of the people, then and then only shall they bring out their wrong doctrines</u>. Therefore I say that you should not give your hearts to men, nor hold people's persons in admiration or adulation. For <u>by these very</u>

persons Satan shall gain entry into My people. Watch for seducers! Do you think a seducer will brandish a heresy and flaunt it before the people? He will speak words of righteousness and truth and will appear as a minister of light, declaring the Word. The people's hearts shall be won. Then when the hearts are won, they will bring out their doctrines and the people shall be deceived. The people shall say 'Did he not speak thus and thus'? 'And did we not examine it from the Word'? 'Therefore he is a minister of righteousness. This that he has now spoken we do not see in the Word but it must be right, for the other things he spoke were true'.

Be not deceived. For the deceiver will first work to gain the hearts of many, and then shall bring forth his insidious doctrines. You cannot discern those who are of Me and those who are not of Me when they start to preach. But seek Me constantly, and then when these doctrines are brought out you shall have a witness in your heart that these are not of Me. Fear not, for I have warned you. Many will be deceived. (The entire prophecy is available on sermonindex .net, and my website: michaelfortner. com)

In the first paragraph quoted it says God will *"purify and sift"* his people with these false teachers. The *Cambridge Dictionary* meaning of the word "sift" is:

to make a close examination of all the parts of something in order to find something or to separate what is useful from what is not:

The definition continued with an example:

The police are trying to sift out the genuine warnings from all the hoax calls they have received.

In other words, God will weed out those who will follow after a personality, a well-known minister, or anointing; or will they follow the truth? Even signs and wonders are not proof that you are following a true minister of God:

God has allowed the WOF teachers and prosperity gospel as a sifting; it only draws those who desire the material things of the world. They <u>do not desire to take up their cross and follow Christ</u>, they prefer wealth. They are not true seekers of God.

In 1965, Hagin had a 15-minute radio program across the nation. The worst he taught was his prosperity gospel, it was the same with Copeland who began preaching in 1967. Neither he or Hagin then taught that the death of Jesus on the cross did not pay for your sins, and that Jesus had to be born-again in hell. But this heresy they did teach <u>after they became influential through TBN,</u> which began in 1973.

If Hagin had taught his lies about Jesus back in the 1950s and 60s, they would have kicked him off the Christian radio stations, which were and are still mostly, <u>not</u> controlled by WOF. It was some time between the mid-1970s to early 90s that Hagin and Copeland began teaching their gross heresy.

Notice that the prophecy said that God will anoint these false ministers. Even though they are mostly powerless, some of them do have a strong anointing, but that does not prove that their doctrines are accurate. God told us in Deut. 13 that he gives dreams and visions and prophecies to people who teach false doctrines, which equates to anointing. And he does this because he is "testing" his followers to see if they will really follow him, or follow the dreams and visions and prophecies. So "testing" is the same as "sifting."

I saw a video of Kenneth Hagin at a big conference in 1997; he got behind the pulpit to teach but could not speak <u>because of a powerful "anointing" on him</u>. So he just walked around touching people, which caused them to laugh, jerk, shake, and fall down, or <u>slither out of their seats to the floor like snakes</u>.

I inquired of God about it, and the thought came to me that no beneficial ministry took place. There was no Gospel preached, no conviction of sin, no salvations, no baptisms in the Holy Spirit, no Bible teaching, no healings-- which means it was nothing but a bless-me counterfeit revival meeting. People can be slain in the Spirit, or jerk and laugh when the Holy Spirit comes upon them, which is shown in the Pentecostal newspapers of the early 20th century. But shaking, jerking, and laughing <u>were all that happened</u> in Hagin's meeting. This is exactly what Stanley Frodsham predicted; *anointed false teachers.*

However, God caused Hagin to engage in some "<u>negative manifestations,</u>" which are intended to expose the error. I suspect I may have coined that term! On the video you can see him flick his tongue several times in and out and around, just like a snake. One time might have been just wetting his lips, but he did it four times in one minute, then a few minutes later he sticks it out real far, flicking it all around. I have the video showing the flicks on my Youtube and Rumble channels. The video also has clips of Ken Copeland making some of his false statements.

Rodney Howard Browne is another "anointed" WOF minister; he can prophesy and even get people healed, but I have seen him on video speaking in what must be fake tongues. He is good buddies with Kenneth Copeland, lives in a multimillion dollar home; and eye witnesses testify that people in his meetings sometimes bark like dogs and meow like cats. <u>This is more "negative manifestations" which God is causing to warn people that the teachings of that minister are false</u>. There were NO REPORTS of barking or meowing among the genuine outpouring of the Spirit 100+ years ago. Though there were some barking or roaring that took place under John Wesley, but he immediately recognized it as being from the devil, and that it was just an attempt to disrupt his meetings.

Sorry, but this is as clear as I could get it.

They also barked and clucked at the Lakeland revival of Todd Bentley that ended in scandal.

Though some healings do take place with WOF preachers, often their anointing is powerless; the anointing sometimes can make you believe you have been healed because the symptoms leave you while in the presence of this anointing; but once you go home, the symptoms return (occasionally this can happen in healings of a real healing evangelist, but not often).

Other "signs" of this counterfeit revival can include such wonders as gold dust, angel feathers, and gold fillings in teeth-- BUT they don't automatically follow; those things come when they are <u>specifically prayed for</u>.

In all of the Pentecostal newspapers which I read, which were far more than I could include in the book, *Pentecostal Newspapers: Messengers of an Outpouring;* there was NOT ONE mention of such things as gold dust, or gold fillings. Yet--- a book published in 2013 claims to contain true stories from Azusa Street including stories of *"gold fillings (one with a diamond inset in it) suddenly manifest itself in their mouths,"* (statement of someone who gave it a 1-star review online; not I). But most people love to dream of such false signs and wonders and gave the book many 5-star ratings. The author claims he personally spoke with people back in the 1960s who were at Azusa when they were young! (So why did he wait 50+ years to write the book?)

If any such signs had occurred it would have been covered by the newspaper reporters who were personally there, or at least in the Pentecostal newspapers; but there were no such accounts!

Frank Bartleman was a Holiness preacher who became a Christian journalist by writing for Holiness papers. He was there in Los Angeles with William Seymour before they moved from the house on Bonnie Brae Street to Azusa Street, and was there <u>the entire revival</u>. It was his news reports and those of the *Los Angeles Times* that made the outpouring known worldwide. In 1925, Frank wrote a book called, *How Pentecost Came to Los Angeles,* which was republished several times with different titles. The most recent was *Azusa Street: The Roots of Modern-day Pentecost,* with an introduction by Vinson Synan, a historian, in 1980. There is <u>no mention in this book of any gold teeth</u> or any other of those false signs and wonders.

Stanley H. Frodsham also wrote a book called, *With Signs Following,* in 1928; revised in 1946. It also has <u>no mention of gold teeth, dust</u>, etc. The 2013 book has no verifiable sources; THIS MEANS THAT the 2013 book likely has many LIES in it. It was endorsed by Bill Johnson and Sid Roth.

The reason the devil included lies in that book is to make people believe that those false signs are actually true signs, in the hopes that people will begin looking for more of those false signs; and when they see them, they will be fooled into believing that they are signs of the true working of the Holy Spirit. But it is a LIE FROM THE PIT OF HELL.

I have heard of one legitimate instance of gold dust appearing on the hand of a Christian being persecuted in prison, which was from God to let the man know that God was with him in his suffering (*Satan's False Prophets Exposed*). God's signs come for a reason. Why would God need to give such signs in the USA? Especially when they are just seeking after the signs; they are just looking for some reason to go, "Ooooh, aaah." The miracles in Pentecostal newspapers included several instances of genuine teeth! God healed people's teeth, but not with gold fillings, but *with new real enamel and whole teeth*!

A true minister of God became deceived into believing that these false signs were of God, and so she began to pray that they happen in her services. The gold dust and gold fillings did not just appear in the services of Ruth Ward Heflin, as "signs following;" I saw a video where she prayed for them to happen. When you pray for the signs, you are seeking after the gift and not the giver (in 99% of the cases these are counterfeit signs done by "familiar spirits," Ibid). She taught another fellow how to pray for the signs, and they began to happen in his church; both Ruth and the other fellow died of cancer within months of each other (Ibid). There is a very high chance, 99%, that the ministers who have gold dust and gold teeth are teaching the prosperity gospel; but they also pray specifically for those things to happen. They think they are praying to God, but they are not! The Bible does NOT include gold dust or angels feathers as some of the signs that will follow the believers.

In the ministry of Maria Woodworth Etter, long before Azusa Street, people would go into trances; while in the trances they would see visions of heaven, hell, the coming of Christ, Christ on the cross, etc. When they came out of the trance-visions, they testified about their visions and people believed and were converted. Some scoffers came yelling and causing trouble and would go into a trance, and when they came out they were praising God and got saved. She had no concept or idea that any such thing would happen in her meetings until they started happening; they were the workings of the Holy Spirit.

Many of the churches she started from her revivals succeeded, but some did not, because those people were only attending to keep having trance-visions. When the visions stopped, the people stopped attending those churches, with the complaint that the pastor did not have the power with him that Sister Etter did. They were seeking the gift and not the giver. At least the people were seeking real manifestations of the real Holy Spirit, and not those worked by false spirits, which have little redeeming purpose.

I believe the Apostle Peter prophesied about the WOF movement:

> . . . there will be false teachers among you. They will <u>secretly introduce destructive heresies</u>, even denying the sovereign Lord who bought them—bringing swift destruction on themselves. Many will follow their depraved conduct and will <u>bring the way of truth into disrepute</u>. In their <u>greed these teachers will exploit you</u> with fabricated stories. Their

condemnation has long been hanging over them, and their destruction has not been sleeping. (2 Peter 2:1-3) (MEV)

I once prayed that God would bring down the WOF movement, but the Jehovah's Witnesses are still around; so are the Mormons. So I now pray for a clear separation between Pentecostals and WOF; while still hoping for the fall of the WOF.

Of course, the WOF movement is not the only thing that has weakened the Pentecostals; there are other factors, but it is not the point of this book to deal with this subject. For more on the general spiritual decline of Christianity, see books and videos by David Wilkerson.

The Pentecostal Church faces many enemies today trying to suppress and supplant it, but until it faces the enemy within, it will not be able to successfully repel the attacks from without. I believe God wants to bring another outpouring of the Spirit; but the cancer of WOF needs to be decisively cut from the Pentecostals and Charismatics who believe in the historic doctrines of Christianity. The WOF must be called what it is, a false cult as bad as Mormonism or Jehovah's Witness.

Would you invite a Jehovah's Witness to speak in your church if they believed in speaking in tongues? But the tongues the WOF teaches is FAKE; the Jesus they teach is just an ordinary man who was born again in hell. THIS IS NOT CHRISTIANITY! One has to question the wisdom and intelligence of any Pentecostal preacher who associates with WOF wolves in sheep's clothing!

Stay away from churches and ministers that teach that Christians *should be wealthy*, or promise a hundred-fold return for an offering. The early Pentecostals had many examples in their papers of how God did NOT need to supply a pile of money for a preacher to do something great for Him; it only takes following God and trusting Him, and God will supply whatever is needed -- NOT a million dollars more than what is needed so the preacher can live in a multi-million-dollar mansion! If God supplies millions of dollars, it is for the many needs that exist within his body; NOT so the money can be spent on a palace.

Someone might say, what about the fact that some WOF ministers seem to get answers to prayers, and get people healed, at least occasionally? Some Roman Catholic priests can also get answers to prayers and get people healed; and some even have miracles, but that does not mean that God is giving full sanction to their doctrines! God can be found in many different churches, but that does not mean that God thereby approves of all their doctrines. Some Pentecostals are Oneness, so they do not believe in the Trinity; but God still works among them. They are far closer to the full truth than any WOF preacher.

A more recent prophetic word was given by Timothy V. Dixon in 2022. He saw two great giants rise up in the land. The first one he called David, just for identification purposes. The second one he called Goliath. The first one was genuine; the second was a false, copy of the first:

> I had a dream . . . such a move of God that it was sweeping the whole Earth; but there were false, false revivals that were trying to raise up and act like that it was the real deal. . . .
>
> I saw two giants . . . a humongous man that could not be defeated. But I also seen another giant that stood up in the land, it looked just exactly like the previous giant . . .
>
> And David stood up in the land through many prophecies of the power of God . . . and you seen great, great, great, moves that has never been done before. Then you seen Goliath standing up, and when Goliath stood up, it was false. It mimicked and it tried to act like David, . . . it looked exactly like David . . . I saw a scattering coming, the real Apostles are not going to be scattered, they are not going to be shook, but the false, there is a false teaching, there is a false manifestation going on right now, that it's going to make a lot of people be scattered because of what we are fixing to face. . . .

(9/26/22 *Prophetic The Gathering of the Last Harvest*, Youtube, Timothy Dixon channel.)

Timothy interpreted this prophecy to refer to the present-day prophetic movement; the true prophets and the false prophets. But they are not giants in the world.

I believe the David giant refers to the Pentecostal outpouring of over 100 years ago, and the second movement that mimicked the true was the Word of Faith movement. They are both giants in the land, but this prophetic word indicates that the counterfeit is going to be scattered!

* * * * * * *

The vision tells us that Satan will attack the Pentecostals from the inside; which represents false doctrines from Satan that will cause many people to lay down their spiritual weapons, and become defeated. This has happened to many Pentecostal people, and whole churches. The Pentecostal church I grew up attending, spoke out against Charismatic doctrines in the early 1970s, but 40 years later it was teaching those doctrines! The main means of infiltration were TBN, Oral Roberts' and Kenneth Copeland's TV shows, and a few others.

The two prophecies confirm the vision. They all point directly to the Word of Faith movement.

Chapter Three

Pentecostal Newspapers

In this chapter I have selected a few articles and testimonies from the early Pentecostal newspapers that are representative of those found in the full length book, *Pentecostal Newspapers: Messengers of an Outpouring (Vol. 2)*. You will notice that the signs and wonders and manifestations they had were not barking, roaring, chicken clucking, or tongue flicking. It also shows their great faith and the mighty miracles that took place among them.

* * * * * * *

Vision and Healing:

Sidney, La, Jan. 3, 1913. For almost a year and a half God had been talking to my soul to get fitted up for His work. On Oct. 25 I went to the house of some Pentecostal people to have them pray for my healing from rheumatism, neuralgia and stomach trouble. I WAS INSTANTLY HEALED.

The power of God came upon me and I was ushered away in a vision from about 7 in the evening until 3 in the morning. I went through the crucifixion with Jesus. I saw the Lord coming in a blue vapor-like cloud. I saw the Devil behind big iron bars. He appeared before me two different times during the vision. I saw the world burning up. Jesus showed me some things. Pray for me. -- Oscar Hiatt

NOTE [from the editor of the paper]: You see from what he says it is now about three months since God healed him. He certainly ought to know in that time whether he was really healed or no. -- (*Word and Witness*, Jan., 1913)

God Visiting San Antonio With Mighty Power:

It has pleased our Heavenly Father to grant us a gracious time of refreshing in this city during the past six weeks. Sister Etter has preached the old time Gospel, not with enticing words of man's wisdom, but in the power and demonstration of the Spirit. She has utterly ignored the "Creeds, Theories, and Dogmas of men," and held high "The Blood Stained Banner of King Emanuel," pointing to the bleeding victim of Golgotha as THE ONLY HOPE OF THE RACE.

From the first God set His seal on her work, "Confirming the word with signs and wonders in the name of Jesus." Sinners have been gloriously saved, the sick have been healed, the deaf have received hearing, the lame have been made to walk, and many have received the gift of the Holy Ghost, speaking with tongues as the Spirit gave them utterance.

A Spanish lady, a Catholic, 79 years of age, all crippled up with paralysis, came into the meeting, was saved, healed and filled with the glory of God: her face shining like an angel as she stood on the altar with uplifted hands praising God for saving her soul and healing her body. A man 80 years old, his form all bent with rheumatism for years, a great sinner and Catholic, came [to] the meeting, heard the singing, saw the shining faces, felt the mighty power of God, fell down at the altar under awful conviction, got saved and healed, threw down his stick and ran up and down the isle shouting the praises of God.

Three deaf mutes came into the meeting, came to the altar, were converted, and two of them declared they could hear the saints praising God: And their tongues were loosed to such a degree that they could say, "Glory" and "Praise God" with a loud voice.

Another man came into town, heard about the meeting, came out, heard, saw, and felt the mighty power of God; had faith to be healed, came to the altar dragging a leg that had been stiff for 12 years. Sister Etter prayed for him, commanding him stretch out the lame limb in Jesus' name, and like the lame man at "the beautiful gate" he instantly obeyed, "leaping up," hopping and skipping like a school boy. He climbed upon the altar, clapping his hands, shouting "I'm healed." Leaping down he ran through the isle giving glory to God before all the people.

One aged man, a precious saint of God, living in this city, who for years has been an invalid, suffering from a fall unable to come to the meeting, but was brought in a buggy, was prayed for and God touched him. Now, using his own terms, he "can walk like a man again."

Many miracles have been performed in Jesus' name. People have been healed of Cancer, Tumor, Catarrh, Rheumatism, Diabetes, Consumption, Sore Eyes, and Eating Sores. Lame limbs have been made whole, and deaf ears have been opened. One lady, dying from all appearances with heart failure, was snatched from the very jaws of death. Her form was cold and limp, her eyes glassy, and the death damp stood on her brow. She had bidden all goodbye and was sinking fast when Sister Etter reached her. But, glory be to God, when our sister rebuked "the grim monster," commanding him to loose her grip, and calling to the departing one to come back, she rallied and came forth in the strength of Israel's God. Now more than a week she has been in the meeting, shouting the praises of God.

Beside the mighty miracles of healing God has shown many other signs of his mighty presence, and the soon coming of the Lord. In many ways the Holy Ghost has signified that we were near the end. Some times during the preaching God's power would settle down on the saints till some were melted to tears, others saw wonderful visions of his coming glory. Some times "the hand maiden of the Lord" was held like a statue, unable to utter a word. Other times she stood weeping over the people, while the power of God swept over all like the tide of the great ocean.

Around the altar souls saw visions among the "Candlesticks," holding the Stars in His right hand. Numbers seemed to hear that voice as the sounding of "great waters" and like John fell at his feet as dead. Oh glory! The unsaved, beholding the shining faces of those lying as dead men in the presence of God, wept and said, "These are strange things."

Many saw visions of Jesus coming in the clouds of heaven with power and great glory. Sometimes the Spirit would move like the gentle breeze, fanning every soul with breath of Heaven, then send torrents of weeping over the lost till it seemed to some that the very shades of the dark "tribulation" cloud was casting a shadow all around us. One morning while the Spirit was dealing with the Saints in a marvelous way, suddenly a sister began to speak in a tongue unknown to any one present, but seemed to be calling us forth to battle.

At this same time several in the Spirit were hearing the "tramp, tramp" of a mighty army, and two saw the mighty armies of Heaven riding forth on White Horses. Then the lady who had been speaking in tongues began giving a shout of victory-- and victory was felt in many hearts -- which was taken up by the saints, while the power and Spirit of God settled down upon us until it seemed the whole place was lighted up with the glory and presence of God.

The Spirit has been revealing in many ways that God is sifting out a people from among all the factions, tribes, and kindreds of earth whom He will send forth in love, clothed with power and might to do exploits and wonders in the name of Jesus, giving to the household of faith their portion in this God's due season.

Sister Etter left us Feb. 17th, to hold meetings in San Jose, Cal. . . . Fred Lohmann. (*Word and Witness*, Feb., 1913)

Faulkner, Kansas:

Since the Eureka Springs camp[meeting] we have held meetings at Siloam Springs, Watts, Saylor, South McAlester [OK], and Muskogee [OK]. God blessed in many places. At Muskogee we had a big fight and great victory. Two other meetings were going on in town, but the folks came where the power was falling. Many times the seekers were 3 [levels] deep at the altar. Many got to God.

A doctor, the Red Cross ambulance and 2 policemen with the patrol wagon came one night, but when the doctor saw the man for whom he was called rise shouting and praising God in other tongues he went out and told the rest they were not needed. Praise God. The last day many were baptized in water before a great crowd and that night was the greatest service of all. Now in a great battle at Faulkner. Pray for us. -- J. H. James. (*WaW*, Feb., 1913)

Fairland, Texas:

God is sending mighty, burning conviction on the unsaved. His children are receiving visions of Jesus. Prophecies of great changes coming are being given in such power of the Spirit that we believe they are coming. Signs appear in the heavens -- a streak of fire six inches by six feet. Three more balls of fire. Many other wonders. Saints, look up. Our redemption draweth nigh. God will do great things. -- Annie Morehead. (*Word and Witness*, March, 1913)

Pellagra Healed:

Nine doctors examined my brother in Oklahoma and pronounced it Pellagra, that dreadful incurable disease. He had had it 6 months and was in a dreadful condition. He knew little about the real power of God, but father, mother, a sister, and myself had the baptisms with the Spirit. So father went after him and brought him home.

Soon he began to look away from man and medicine to God. Then later he came to Quannah where are a few Pentecostal saints. It was Christmas time, and we were in meetings. We prayed for him several times during 3 or 4 days, but did not seem to reach the throne. One night after meeting we got down in earnest for him. The heavens opened and the Spirit fell upon us and the power of God struck him like a thunderbolt. It brought him to his feet dancing and praising God, a thing he had never done. He was set free, and took the next train home to tell his wife and children what the Lord had done for him. He left the boy who came with him to care for him in traveling. Jesus went back with him. I have heard from him every two weeks since, and he is still healed and praising God. -- B. L. Richardson, Quannah, Texas. (Ibid)

Revival Fires Beginning, Searcy, Ark.:

Wife and I came here in November, 1915, with our tent and started a meeting. God wonderfully blessed and saved several. Some eight or nine received the baptism of the Spirit. We went to work and built a tabernacle and just closed a three weeks meeting. Nineteen received the baptism of the Spirit and several were saved. The country was stirred. We have a good little band on fire for God and working in unity and love toward each other. Pray for us that God will have His way and that many more souls may be brought to God. -- J. G. Neal, Searcy, Ark. (*The Weekly Evangel*, May 5, 1916)

San Antonio, Texas:

God is wonderfully working in San Antonio among the colored people, a people who have been neglected by Pentecostal people, but thanks be to God, He in due time is visiting this people in mighty power. A large number saved, and 39 baptized in Holy Ghost.

The sick are being raised from their beds and marvelously healed by the power of God. A man who came in the mission two weeks ago with consumption in it's last stage, was healed, saved, and baptized in the Holy Ghost and fire. Now he is witnessing everywhere to the power of God. F. C. V. Foard, from

Hearne, Texas is conducting the meeting, assisted by Bro. C. E. Overstreet and W. M. Burnside, both of Los Angeles, Cal. There is a great battle on, the people are stirred in this place as never before. . . .-- W. M. Burnside. (*Word and Wit.*, May, 1913)

Barnum, Texas:

The fire is falling along the Polk and Tyler county line in the piney woods of Texas. At Caney church 7 have received the baptism and two and one-half miles away at Hampton 10 more received, two preachers in the number, one Methodist and one Baptist. Bro. D. K. Morris and band are at Barnum and fire is falling. A great battle is before us. -- W. E. Cleghorn. (*WaW*, May, 1913)

MIRACLES IN DAILY NEWS:

From the ARIZONA GAZETTE of Saturday, April 19th, I clip the following concerning God's works in Phoenix, Arizona:

"Among the wonderful evidences of God's healing powerful are those manifest at the little Pentecostal mission at the corner of Fifth avenue and Washington street where Rev. M. M. Pinson, an evangelist from Nashville, Tenn. Is conducting a real old time gospel meeting and where signs and wonders are in evidence as in apostolic times.

"Among those from Osborn who have come under the miraculous power of God at this meeting is one of the pupils of Osborn school. Allen Homes, age sixteen, son of R. L. Homes, who was a victim of spinal meningitis about five years ago before coming to Arizona, leaving his left arm and his right leg in a badly paralyzed condition, and therefore was two inches shorter than his other arm. After a faithful, earnest prayer was offered in his behalf the boy was instantly healed by divine power, and the crippled arm now measures the same length as other one.

"D. D. Culbert of 1105 East Pierce street, a painter and paper hanger, had a bad fall two years ago which injured his spine in such a way that only by suffering severe pain could he follow his trade. He was treated by a number of physicians, including an osteopath, without relief, but when he came under the heal- ing power of God through the blood of Christ Jesus he was made well and straight, and is anxious that this be investigated so other sufferers may be led to health and strength and eternal life through Christ Jesus." -- Arizona Gazette. (Ibid)

East Ellijay, GA.:

God is working here in a wonderful way. About 50 souls have been saved. A great number healed and quite a few bap- tized with the Holy Ghost. When we first came here the Meth- odist church was opened to us, but the Presiding Elder came along and said we must not teach the baptism with the Holy Ghost with the sign of speaking in tongues as on the day of Pentecost. Then the Lord opened up a store building for meet- ing where God wonderfully poured out His Spirit saving people and healing the sick; also baptizing with the Holy Ghost.

Then the enemy forced us to leave the store building and God gave us a place of worship of our own. This made the devil madder than ever, and he sent us word to leave town at once. People got so stirred they began to read, walk the streets and quarrel, and threaten my life. One person even placed a stick of dynamite in my back yard where it exploded. Praise God, it hurt no one but put the town in a uproar.

A few days later two sticks [of dynamite] were found under our church fixed to blow it up. The fuses burned out and they failed to go off, so no harm was done. The same day a deacon of one of the churches met me on the street and tried to kill me with a stick. While he was beating me and the blood running down to my feet, Jesus said, "My grace is sufficient." Then when the old deacon saw that he had hurt me he raised up his hands and cried murder, and went and got out a writ of assault under a $100.00 bond for my appearance in court. Well praise God. When the trial came, even my enemies swore that I did not break the law, and I came clear. God gave us the victory. Bless His name.

The second Sunday in May God gave us a wonderful time. We baptized 12 in water. Two of these were Mayor Trammell and his daughter, Miss Pearl. We are expecting a blessed camp-meeting . . . (*WaW*, June, 1913)

Milton, Fla.:

God has wonderfully blessed our evangelistic labors here. He worked with signs and wonders. About 40 have professed Christ as Savior, 19 have been baptized in water and about 33 or 34 have been baptized with the Spirit. More are to follow in the watery burial and symbolic resurrection. Several were healed.

A pillow of fire rested over the tent one night, and another night two large hands waved over it. Both saints and sinners saw the signs. As we shall be here yet some time the brethren may write us at Milton, Fla. -- I. N. Jordon. (*WaW*, Aug., 1913)

Dallas, Texas:

A week ago we moved our tent to a new location in North Dallas. We enlarged it with an extra piece in the center and yet the first night it would not hold the people. The 30 foot altar was filled with sinners seeking the Lord the first night. Some falling under the power were brightly converted and baptized in the Spirit. It has continued this way every night since. Last night's meeting was wonderful.

We baptize the new converts every Sunday at Oak Lawn Park, and big crowds gather to witness these services. Nearly all of the converts come out of the water shouting praises to God. 12 is the smallest number we have baptized at one time. Today an unsaved woman came to the meeting for healing, and was saved, healed and baptized in the Spirit, and went home rejoicing. Our Sunday morning meetings at the main tabernacle are most precious. The saints are joyful, and expecting great things from God. -- F. F. Bosworth. (*WaW*, Sept., 1913)

God's Deeds of Mercy and Power in Chicago:

The meetings here are progressing nicely. Among those healed was a woman who had been blind 15 years and had several children whom she had never seen. She was perfectly healed, so she could see as good as ever.

A man who was paralyzed and whose joints were ossified was brought to the church in a chair. He had no use of his muscles at all, could not move his head or any of his limbs. His speech was almost gone and he had to be fed on liquid food with a spoon. When he was prayed for he jumped up and ran out of the church down the steps and a half block down the street. The next day he was back to testify to his healing and to glorify God. This man had been in this sickness 8 years.

A young lady who was totally deaf in one ear, the drum being destroyed, and was almost deaf in the other ear, having also a terrible abscess behind one of her ears, was prayed for. She has been back several times and testified to her complete healing and the restoration of her hearing. She can hear a watch tick when placed to the ear that had the drum destroyed.

Perhaps 50 people were prayed for today, among who was a girl who was totally blind in both eyes. One eyeball was very large and apparently bulged out, and the other one seemed as if the white and colored parts had run together. When she was prayed for and the Lord began to restore her sight, she became "excited" and jumped and screamed until she fell and when she recovered herself and opened her eyes again and could see the light and distinguish the windows she started in again and was almost guilty of disturbing public worship. But such scenes are so common in these meetings that we are not disturbed by them. -- F. A. Hale. [at The Stone Church] (*WaW*, Aug., 1913)

Notes:

Letters come to us daily telling of blessings received through *The Evangel*, and our hearts are melted in gratitude to God for the blessing He makes it to those who have not Christian fellowship. . . .

Brother Bosworth writes that on a certain Sunday a woman in Dallas who needed healing was reading the article in the June Evangel on "Discerning the Lord's Body," and the power of God fell upon her and she was healed and blessed in her spirit. That night Jesus and an angel appeared to her and Jesus talked to her. (*The Latter Rain Evangel*, Aug., 1914)

Boswell, Oklahoma:

God has been working in these parts again. Just about to close another big meeting. People are wonderfully interested, coming from 8 to 10 miles around. Some have been saved; several received the baptism as in Acts 2:4. Seven or eight hundred present Sunday, which is remarkable for this location.

People have been stirred by some of the things which have been seen. Some saw smoke pouring out of the tent and sent to see who had set it on fire. Upon reaching there they found no fire. One night, as people were returning from meeting, it was dark, but suddenly the heavens were lit up as bright as day. The light went toward the north, and the report that followed it jarred the ground and shook houses. Some began to praise the Lord and others fell down and began to cry and pray for they thought Jesus was coming. Hallelujah! -- J. M. Murray. (*WaW*, Oct., 1914)

[No heading, just *** before the notice:]

Other [Gospel] workers visiting in a hospital met a young German who was very ill. The nurse said there was not much chance for his recovery. He had been in the hospital for five months and was now having spasms. Many times they were so severe he would throw himself out of the bed.

The workers were especially burdened for him and the Lord dealt with his soul. He consecrated his life to God and promised Him he would work for Him if He would heal his body.

The Lord answered his prayer and restored him. He afterwards came to the Stone Church and received a wonderful baptism. He had a vision of Jesus standing among the angels with a golden scepter in his hand. Before coming to this country he was a socialist preacher for two years. His parents had cast him off but after he was saved they assured him he would be welcome in their home. (*The Latter Rain Evangel*, Feb., 1914)

A Remarkable Vision and Testimony of Healing:

I thank God for His loving Holy Spirit that dwells with us all the time.

The angel of the Lord showed me the Holy City that John saw coming down from heaven one night when I was praying at my little home. I went into the Holy City in a vision and I saw the seven angels standing before the throne of God with their trumpets ready to sound. God had taken His seat on the throne and I saw, on the trumpet of the first angel written that the end should come in 19__. The angel showed me my crown and it was beautiful. It had 130 stars in it. The Holy City was made of pure gold as clear as crystal. . . . -- L. G. Chandler, Colt, Arkansas. (*The Weekly Evangel,* March 28, 1914)

***

While a young man was driving a nail it flew into his eyeball, making an incision on the edge of the pupil. He was taken to the hospital and his eye was scraped. At first the doctor thought it would be restored, but in a few days it grew rapidly worse. The physician said the ball of the eye was soft and would have to be taken out; that if allowed to remain in, it would affect the other eye.

The young man had been somewhat unconcerned up to this time, but when he realized it was serious he became quite exercised to the Divine Healing meeting on a Wednesday afternoon and as he was anointed with oil and prayer offered, a number of the workers were specifically burdened for his healing. The power of God came upon him and flooded him. He felt the fire of God penetrate the eye and the pain left. He believed the Lord healed him then.

He was obliged to see the physician the next day who was astonished to find him so much better and told him he would not now need to have the eye removed. His eye is practically healed, and he can now see from it.

He speaks enthusiastically of the great spiritual blessing he received at the Divine Healing meeting. He said the Lord gave him a fresh baptism and flooded his soul with glory. (*TLRE*, Aug., 1915, page 14)

Signs Following in Milwaukee:

Evangelist Hard W. Mitchell, who spent several weeks in Milwaukee, Wisconsin, gives us a few items of interest concerning the revival being conducted there by the Pastor C. B. Fockler, assisted by Brother Bosworth, E. N. Richey and other brethren:—

The Lord placed His seal of approval on the first service by wonderfully healing a man who had been hurt and left crippled by an automobile. An account of his healing was published in the secular press the next morning.

The saints were inspired to believe for a heavenly influence to settle down on the place and for every sinner to be affected by it. It has been as they believed; with very few exceptions, every sinner who came into the meeting has been convicted and converted.

A woman was brought out of her sick bed and carried into the meeting. She had a tumor and had not been able to eat anything for three months except orange juice and a little baby food. The moment hands were laid on her she was healed and baptized in the Holy Spirit. Her first meal after her healing consisted of beefsteak and biscuits. She has been at each meeting since, testifying to what the Lord has done for her.

A little boy who was brought in a wheelchair was instantly healed, and was able to run all over the place. He is walking alright now.

The altar has been filled continually with from fifteen to fifty. Many of these are Lutherans and Roman Catholics and God is saving and baptizing them. Sunday night, July 25, we had a most wonderful meeting. At least seventy-five came to the altar; eleven were struck down by the power of God and held for hours with visions of heaven and hell, and given warnings for the unsaved.

Miss Jessie Wengler, who is an active worker in the revival, sends us the following report:

"Like the olden times when they heard that Jesus was to 'pass that way,' they thronged Him, some but to touch the hem of His garment. So night after night in Milwaukee, hungry and thirsty souls press their claims and many have rejoiced at the touch from His hand, many have tasted and found that the Lord is good.

"Sweet assurance was given to some whose hearts had been doubtful. One young lady who had never felt quite sure that her name was written in the Lamb's Book of Life, while praying was carried away in the Spirit and walked the streets of gold. Jesus led her to the Lamb's Book, and opened it and handed her a golden pen. He asked her to write her name, which she did in letters of pure gold. Her soul was flooded with glory and her doubts vanished.

"A poor woman in the depths of despondency -- her husband blind and a drunkard, she a cripple, paralyzed from the hips down, wasting away with consumption and walking with the aid of crutches, was on her way to the river to drown herself. Hearing the singing at the street-meeting, she stopped. They sang and talked about Jesus and His power to save and heal. Instead of going to the river she came to the meeting at the Hall and plunged into the life-giving current that never runs dry. She found the stream that flows from Calvary sufficient for all her sins and all her diseases, and went away without the aid of her crutches, leaning on the arm of Jesus and filled with that peace that passeth understanding." (*The Latter Rain Evangel*, Aug., 1915, page 14-15)

Opp. Alabama; A Heavenly Visitation:

God is still working in this section with signs and wonders. We have just closed a meeting at Opine. God [worked] wonderfully one night during praise service and let down the Heavenly Host to play and sing for us. Many of the saints and many sinners heard the heavenly choir. Lights were seen over and above the tent. Sinners were saved and believers filled with the Spirit and the saints refreshed. Many gainsayers were convinced.

Bro. G. S. McGraw of Georgiana, Ala. was with us. We appreciated his presence and labor. We have found no place to halt or camp in this race but our hearts are open for new truths. We believe God has great things laid up in store for those that obey Him and who wholly follow the Lord. Josh. 14:6-14. Pray for us. -- A. B. Robinson and wife. (*Word and Wit.*, Oct., 1915)

His Glorious Power Manifested:

I am praising God for the wonderful outpouring of His Spirit which He gave us at Runge, Texas. Bro. Short, myself and wife held a three weeks meeting and the Lord was with us in power and great glory. Twenty were baptized in water, all having been saved or reclaimed, with the exception of three or four. Eighteen received the baptism in the Holy Spirit as in Acts 2:4, with signs and wonders following.

Some had visions of the heavens opened up. Others saw angels rejoicing about them, while still others had a glimpse of our blessed Savior Himself. I have attended some glorious meetings since I have been out [working] for the Lord, but I must say, I have never seen the spirit of joy manifested so greatly heretofore as I have seen it in this place. Pray for us that God will be with us in our next place. -- D. W. Edwards. (*The Weekly Evangel*, July 1, 1916)

　　***

I remember one convention we had in South China when the power of the Spirit was being poured out, and the Lord was slaying the natives on every hand; our hearts felt repaid for every hardship to see natives being baptized in the Holy Spirit. Our Bible woman from Waang Kong was praising the Lord in other tongues, and suddenly she began to sing in the Spirit. We stole closely to her and she was singing in clear English, "The angels are surrounding me," with a rapt expression on her face. I thought if those who have been opposed to Pentecost could see this native woman who did not know any English, singing in clear, perfect English in the holy hush of the Spirit's presence, it would have removed all their opposition. (*The Latter Rain Evangel*, June, 1918, page 22-23)

    ***

This morning while at family worship my ten year old daughter was carried off in the Spirit. She was just like dead for about half an hour, and when she came back she said she had seen a beautiful city coming down out of heaven, and a great light back of it, and an angel before it. All glory to God, He is making revelations to His people. -- F. A. Woodlawn. (*The Pentecostal Evangel,* March, 1921, page 5)

* * * * * * *

If you are WOF and want to know the truth about historic Christianity, I recommend you purchase a book on basic Christianity, and/or Pentecostal doctrines. For example: *Mere Christianity*, by C.S. Lewis; and *Knowing the Doctrines of the Bible*, by Myer Pearlman.

P.S. Just to be clear, even though there are no quotes included in this book about laughter, the early Pentecostals did occasionally experience Holy Laughter. But if that is all that happens in a service, just a whole bunch of laughter and no salvations, then that is not a genuine revival. It is just a bless-me revival, and does not resemble any of the thousands that took place in the Pentecostal outpouring of 100+ years ago.

CPSIA information can be obtained
at www.ICGtesting.com
Printed in the USA
BVHW081048230123
656900BV00002B/132